got all my sisters with me. We are family, g[...]ee we're

the people around us they say, can they b[...]d, we're

body and sing! Living life is fun and we've j[...]delights.

ed, here's what we call our golden rule. Hav[...]on't go

body and sing! We are family, I got all my sisters with me. We are family, get up everybody and

can see we're together, as we walk on by. (FLY!) and we fly just like birds of a feather, I won't

he record, we're giving love in a family dose. We are family, I got all my sisters with me. We are

orld's delights. (HIGH!) high hopes we have for the future, and our goal's in sight. (WE!) no we

you won't go wrong, this is our family jewel. We are family, I got all my sisters with me. We are

everybody and sing! We are family, I got all my sisters with me. We are family, get up everybody

eather, I won't tell no lie. (ALL!) all of the people around us they say, can they be that close. Just

h me. We are family, get up everybody and sing! Living life is fun and we've just begun, to get

t. (WE!) no we don't get depressed, here's what we call our golden rule. Have faith in you and

h me. We are family, get up everybody and sing! We are family, I got all my sisters with me. We

t up everybody and sing! Everyone can see we're together, as we walk on by. (FLY!) and we fly

e that close. Just let me state for the record, we're giving love in a family dose. We are family, I

begun, to get our share of the world's delights. (HIGH!) high hopes we have for the future, and

h in you and the things you do, you won't go wrong, this is our family jewel. We are family, I got

with me. We are family, get up everybody and sing! We are family, I got all my sisters with me.

!) and we fly just like birds of a feather, I won't tell no lie. (ALL!) all of the people around us they

e are family, I got all my sisters with me. We are family, get up everybody and sing! Living life is

r the future, and our goal's in sight. (WE!) no we don't get depressed, here's what we call our

e are family, I got all my sisters with me. We are family, get up everybody and sing! We are fam-

y sisters with me. We are family, get up everybody and sing! Everyone can see we're together,

WE ARE FAMILY!

**Andrews McMeel
Publishing**

Kansas City

CD included featuring Sister Sledge

Photographs by Steve Bloom Images

We are family,

I got all my

sisters with me.

We are family,

get up everyb

...ody and sing!

We are family,

I got all my

sisters with me.

We are family,

get up everybody

and sing!

Everyone can

see we're together,

as we **walk** on by.

(FLY!) and we fly just like birds of a feather,

I won't tell no lie.

(ALL) all of the people around us they say,

can they be

that close?

Just let me state for the record,

we're giving love

in a family dose.

We are family,

I got all my sisters with me.

We are family,

get up everybody and sing!

Living life is fun...

and we've just begun,

to get our share of the

world's delights.

(HIGH!)

high hopes we have for the future,

and our goal's in sight.

(WE!) no we don't get depressed,

here's what we call

our golden rule.

Have faith in you

and the things you do, you won't go wrong,

this is our family jewel.

We are family, I got all my sisters with me.

We are family, get up everybody and sing!

We are family, I got all my sisters with me. We are family, get up everybody and sing! We are fa

together, as we walk on by. (FLY!) and we fly just like birds of a feather, I won't tell no lie. (ALL!

giving love in a family dose. We are family, I got all my sisters with me. We are family, get up

(HIGH!) high hopes we have for the future, and our goal's in sight. (WE!) no we don't get dep

wrong, this is our family jewel. We are family, I got all my sisters with me. We are family, get up

sing! We are family, I got all my sisters with me. We are family, get up everybody and sing! Eve

tell no lie. (ALL!) all of the people around us they say, can they be that close. Just let me state

family, get up everybody and sing! Living life is fun and we've just begun, to get our share of

don't get depressed, here's what we call our golden rule. Have faith in you and the things you

family, get up everybody and sing! We are family, I got all my sisters with me. We are family, ge

and sing! Everyone can see we're together, as we walk on by. (FLY!) and we fly just like birds o

let me state for the record, we're giving love in a family dose. We are family, I got all my siste

our share of the world's delights. (HIGH!) high hopes we have for the future, and our goal's in

the things you do, you won't go wrong, this is our family jewel. We are family, I got all my siste

are family, get up everybody and sing! We are family, I got all my sisters with me. We are fami

just like birds of a feather, I won't tell no lie. (ALL!) all of the people around us they say, can th

got all my sisters with me. We are family, get up everybody and sing! Living life is fun and we'v

our goal's in sight. (WE!) no we don't get depressed, here's what we call our golden rule. Hav

all my sisters with me. We are family, get up everybody and sing! We are family, I got all my s

We are family, get up everybody and sing! Everyone can see we're together, as we walk on by

say, can they be that close. Just let me state for the record, we're giving love in a family dose

fun and we've just begun, to get our share of the world's delights. (HIGH!) high hopes we ha

golden rule. Have faith in you and the things you do, you won't go wrong, this is our family jew

ily, I got all my sisters with me. We are family, get up everybody and sing! We are family, I got